Happily Ever After

THE FAIRY-TALE FORMULA

FOR LASTING LOVE

HarperResource

An Imprint of

HarperCollins*Publishers*

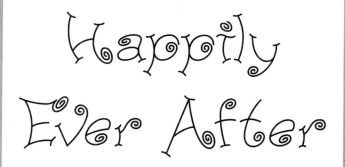

Happily Ever After

THE

FAIRY-TALE FORMULA

FOR LASTING LOVE

WENDY PARIS

FIRST EDITION

Designed by Claire Vaccaro

Library of Congress Cataloging-in-Publication Data
Paris, Wendy.
   Happily ever after : the fairy tale formula for lasting love / by Wendy Paris.
      p.   cm.
   ISBN 0-06-620972-2 (hardcover)
      1. Man-woman relationships.   2. Mate selection.   3. Women—Psychology.
      I. Title.

HQ801.P325 2002
306.7—dc21

                                                                2001039028

01   02   03   04   05   RRD   10   9   8   7   6   5   4   3   2   1

To my mother, Joy King,
for showing me how to treat people well

contents

x

acknowledgments

There are few things I'm proud of that I really made all by myself. When I look at any of my personal success stories, I see a team of people who helped—not just through practical, physical means, but also in less concrete ways. Introducing me to someone. Proofreading with all their might. Assuming my competence before I've really proven it.

Eternal thanks to my office mate and current favorite novelist, Sharon Krum, for brainstorming about relationship-book ideas and hitting on the winning one, as well as encouraging me to proceed. Thanks to my agent, Barbara J. Zitwer, for her passion for this project, excellent guidance, and astute input. Many thanks to Marjorie Braman at HarperCollins for making this project so enjoyable from start to finish. It's rare to find an editor who is as enthusiastic about your book as you are and consistently respectful of your vision. Thanks to Otto Steininger for working so hard to create the spare yet conceptually complex illustrations, and to Karen Salmansohn for suggesting him. Thanks to Leah Carlson-Stanisic and all of the design team at HarperCollins for taking so much care with the look of the book.

Many thanks to Joy King and Sandy Raitt for proofreading and rereading (and rereading) the manuscript and spending hours discussing the vagaries of relationships and fairy tales. Thanks to Jessie Klein, David Callahan, Jessica O'Brien, and Sara Clemence for additional proofreading.

Last but not least, thanks to all the gallant men I've known. Men who act according to their own codes of conduct, casting utopian spheres of personal decency into what can be a vulgar and abrading world—particularly Leonard Porter, my model of contemporary chivalry, and David Callahan, my prince.

Happily

Ever After

THE FAIRY-TALE FORMULA

FOR LASTING LOVE

Introduction

ove is a battlefield." "Men are dogs." "It's a jungle out there." These common views pit men and women against each other, presenting dating as war and the road to love as a treacherous pass filled with land mines and quicksand. An hour spent in a bookstore's dating section is enough to convince any single woman that she's destined to be alone forever unless she can craft the perfect strategy to land a man, employing the coquetry of a southern belle, mapped out on a battle plan devised by an army general, under the guidance of a fleet of psychologists trained in manipulation.

This popular prescription suggests that waging emotional war is the route to a peaceful union, that the only way to "get" a man is to make him fear he can't get you. Strategic dating implies that *what* you do is more important than *whom* you do it with, that the individual doesn't matter, that the wrong man can be sculpted into the right man if you wield your chisel right.

There's one problem with this tactical approach to falling in love. It doesn't work.

There isn't one strategy to finding and keeping a man. Every person is different. Each relationship evolves according to its own rules. People's histories and hangups vary. Luck and timing come into play. Fate unfolds unexpectedly. Dating is too unpredictable to be mastered with one grand plan.

Which is a lot like the world of fairy tales. Fairy tales come from prescientific times, when daily life seemed enigmatic and ever changing. Fairy-tale heroines are always finding themselves locked in towers or cast from home, required to make difficult choices based on arbitrary conditions, left to rely on people who change into animals, and vice versa.

Contrary to popular belief, fairy-tale heroines are not weak and passive. For the most part, they are noble, brave, and optimistic. You'll never find a fairy-tale heroine moping around the house, cursing the fates for having orphaned her with a jealous, shallow stepmother. Fairy-tale heroines don't waste time obsessing about whether or not they were too friendly to the handsome prince. They know their actions can't determine the behavior of others. They don't try to manipulate people or events. Instead, they focus on what they can control—their own character. They have found the formula for success in a chaotic world: holding fast to their own beliefs, no matter what fate throws their way. Ultimately, it is their strong, unflinching moral center—their character—that saves them, not the prince on the white horse.

These age-old tales have a lot to teach us if we look at them in a new light. Each chapter in this book offers a new interpretation of a classic fairy tale, highlighting the ways in which the heroines maintain their moral center and end up madly in love. Fairy tales highlight the value of treating others with respect and kindness, characteristics that often seem overlooked in today's more cynical search for love.

Fairy tales also suggest a more merciful view of others and oneself than is common in today's dating world. Friends often call me with the details of their dates, sure they said "the wrong thing" or made "a wrong move" that will drive the guy away. Tales such as "Thumbelina" and "Grace and Derek" show that there is no "one wrong move." People in fairy tales often make mistakes. It's impossible to be perfect when the world around you isn't. But they always learn from their mistakes, continue trying to be their best, and wind up happy in the end.

The book also includes three tales of warning that show the result of failing to follow the fairy-tale formula. While I've pinpointed one primary piece of advice to glean from each tale, they all offer more than one lesson. You may find that a different aspect of a story relates more specifically to you and your search for your prince.

And don't let anyone tell you that the handsome prince no longer exists. As a recent rearrival on the singles scene, I've been amazed to discover just how princelike men can be. There's a gallantry among men that the strategic dating books don't acknowledge. There is chivalry out there, if you have the confidence to accept it and the strength to know that being treated like a princess does not make you a slave.

By taking the fairy-tale approach to dating—keeping your values and facing the vagaries of relationship building with unflinching optimism and courage—you go a long way toward ensuring that the road to your castle is smooth and that when your handsome prince comes along, you'll see him.

First paint a cage
with an open door
then paint
something pretty
something simple
something beautiful
something useful
for the bird
then place the canvas against a tree
in a garden
in a wood
or in a forest
hide behind the tree
without saying anything
without moving . . .
Sometimes the bird comes quickly
but it is possible for him to wait years
before he decides
Don't be discouraged

wait

wait if necessary for years

whether the bird comes fast or slow

has no

bearing

on the success of the picture

When the bird arrives

should he arrive

observe the most profound silence

wait until the bird enters the cage

and at that stage

shut the door gently with a putt of the brush

wipe out one by one all the bars

careful not to touch any of the bird's feathers

Then paint the tree

choosing the most beautiful branches

for the bird

paint too the green foliage and the freshness of
the wind

the dust of the sun
the noise of insects in the grass in the summer
    heat
and then wait until the bird decides to sing
If the bird doesn't sing
it's a bad sign
a sign that the painting is bad
but if he sings it's a good sign
sign that you may sign
Then pull out very gently
one of the feathers of the bird and write your
    name in a corner of the picture.

—"To Make the Portrait of a Bird,"

by Jacques Prevert, translated by

Harriet Zinnes

CHAPTER ONE

Cinderella

ORPHANED BEAUTY
DRESSES FOR SUCCESS,
SEIZES CHANCE FOR CHANGE

inderella, as beautiful inside as out, is left at the mercy of her malicious stepmother and two stepsisters upon the death of her father. They treat her like a maid.

The king throws the bash of the millennium. Of course, Cinderella isn't invited. Evil step-relations exploit her considerable artistic skills to help them doll up for the big event.

Enter Fairy Godmother, an Old World fashion consultant–cum–magician who magically transforms Cinderella into Claudia Schiffer in a Valentino dress. A random pumpkin becomes a Porsche, and Cinderella races to the ball.

The prince gets one look at Cinderella and forgets about all the other girls in the kingdom. He asks her to dance every number. At midnight, Cinderella cuts out, per Fairy Godmother's orders. She's in such a rush that she doesn't retrieve the glass slipper that has fallen from her foot.

The prince is devastated by her departure. It's as if her image has been burned on his brain. He sends his assistants all over town with the glass slipper, looking for Cinderella. They go door to door, chanting, "If the shoe fits, he will commit."

Everyone wants to be a millionaire. But the slipper fits only Cinderella. The prince rushes to her fireside and whisks her off to live happily ever after.

❖ ❖ ❖ ❖ ❖ ❖ ❖ ❖

The most commonly told version of "Cinderella" was published in 1697 by the French intellectual Charles Perrault (using

his ten-year-old son's name as a pseudonym).
Perrault was the first to record many of the
well-known fairy tales of European oral tradi-
tion. The story may have originated in China,
where a small foot was a sign of beauty.

◆ ◆ ◆ ◆ ◆ ◆ ◆ ◆

Cinderella

THE SAVVY DATER READING

Yes, Cinderella had the worst job in the city, but she did it diligently. She didn't waste hours in useless rancor, letting bitterness and regret give her an ulcer, bad skin, and deep brow furrows. She knew "cinder maid" was just her job title, not her life description.

When the fairy godmother appeared, Cinderella had the courage to seize an opportunity to change. She didn't peer at the fairy godmother suspiciously, snarling, "You know what they say, 'If something looks too good to be true, it probably is.' Leave me to my cinders. I'm perfectly happy with my state of habitual discontent." Cinderella knew she was worthy of happiness, despite a string of bad luck so long, a lesser woman would have hanged herself with it.

*O*nce she arrived at the ball, Cinderella didn't hide inside her pumpkin carriage, crying, "But no one attends a party alone! Everyone will think I'm a loser!" She threw her shoulders back, lifted her chin, and marched in the door.

*C*inderella believed in the power of a perfect dress.

*S*he did not waste time gloating over her step-siblings in her designer duds. She knew that the best revenge is having too much fun to think about retaliation.

*W*hen the prince asked her to dance, Cinderella did not shriek and run to the ladies' room to check her lipstick. She agreed to dance. And you can bet that while spinning in his arms, she didn't trip into a fit of insecurity, criticizing him in an attempt to boost her self-esteem, saying, "You know, anyone can inherit a kingdom. I *work* for my living."

At the stroke of midnight, she didn't cling to the prince's hand, crying, "Save me from my miserable life!" She had the confidence to know that if he liked her, he'd come calling.

Which, of course, he did. And when he came, she did not listen to her friends, who all rang up, saying, "Why is he shooting so far beneath his mark, Cinderella? I mean, no offense, but what's wrong with him that none of the royal chicks will date him?" She knew the details of her relationship better than her friends did, trusting her own experience with her man, not gossip.

When the prince galloped up on his white horse, Cinderella did not shout, "Hey man, back off! I can drive my own damn steed!" She decided that if it was that important to him to whisk her off her feet, she'd let him whisk.

Cinderella

RELATIONSHIP RULES, IN BRIEF

☀ Know your inner value, no matter how worth-less your external situation may seem.

☀ If something looks too good to be true, it can still be true.

☀ Don't be afraid to go to a party alone.

☀ Never underestimate the power of dressing your best.

☀ Focus on finding your own happiness, not on avenging past slights.

☀ Get out on the dance floor!

☀ Don't let your own insecurity drive you to criticize others.

☀ Keep your obligations and promises to others, even if some handsome guy wants you to dance all night.

☀ Ignore rumors and doubts of suspicious friends. Judge a person based on your own experience with him.

☀ Work on becoming your own best adviser.

☀ If a man wants to sweep you off your feet, go ahead and let him. Just because he's gallant doesn't mean he wants you to quit your job and take up knitting.

Fairy-tale Formula
Rule 1:

Don't let past bad luck cloud

your vision of a brighter future.

Have the courage to believe

in a better life.

CHAPTER TWO

The Princess and the Pea

ROYAL PAIN SNAGS PRINCE BY
SHOWING TRUE SELF

here's a prince who wants to get married. He dates every princess on the planet, but no one meets his precise (if somewhat wacky) standards of "real" princessness.

Back home, depressed, moping about the castle on a rainy night, he hears a knock on the door. Standing in the rain, dripping wet head to toe, is a young woman who claims to be a real princess.

The king and queen take her in for the night. The queen decides to test the self-proclaimed princess to see if she is the real deal. She puts a pea under the mattress in the guest room, piling twenty mattresses on top of the pea, and twenty eiderdown comforters on top of those.

In the morning, when asked how she slept, the princess complains about a lump in her bed that kept her up all night, bruising her black-and-blue. (She doesn't, oddly enough, complain about being forced to sleep high atop a weaving tower of bedding.)

Oh, she's so sensitive as to feel a pea beneath all those mattresses! She must be a real princess! (The prince decides.) At last! And when least expected! The prince marries her and they live happily, if oversensitively, ever after.

◆ ◆ ◆ ◆ ◆ ◆ ◆

W ritten by Hans Christian Andersen and published in Danish in 1835, "The Princess and the Pea" is based on a folk tale that Andersen heard as a child. The son of a poor cobbler and a washerwoman, Andersen was keenly interested in the concept of inherent nobility despite an outward appearance of poverty.

❖ ❖ ❖ ❖ ❖ ❖ ❖ ❖

The Princess and the Pea

THE SAVVY DATER READING

*O*kay, this is a ridiculous story. You don't show up, uninvited and dripping wet, at someone's castle, demanding accommodations. It's not only rude, but it also suggests a myriad of personal problems. Why are you wandering around in the rain alone in the middle of the night? Did your parents/boyfriend/cellmates kick you out? Did you forget to take your medicine, an omission that sent you running headlong into the rain in a psychotic fit? Are you a clever thief who relies on inclement weather and your own waifish charm as tools of entry? What dysfunction *do* you have?

Not only that, if the castle owners overlook the obvious warning signs and offer you respite for the night, don't spend the breakfast hour complaining about your bedroom. If you're begging for bedding, you can't expect the Ritz. Especially when you arrive without a gift for your hosts. This princess had deplorable manners.

That's my opinion, but obviously not the prince's. He had his own ideas about what makes a person a princess—hypersensitivity to barely discernible objects, for example, rather than a sunny disposition or appropriate gratitude.

The princess showed up at the castle and claimed royal birth, despite looking like a runaway. She didn't have snapshots of her moat and drawbridge or a glittery crown on her head. But she had the confidence to know that her inner nobility would shine through, even without proof of pedigree.

The princess did not try to modify her behavior—pretending to be easygoing and pleasant, for example—in her efforts to charm the prince. She knew that the right man would love her as she was. He would see her fussiness as a sign of fineness, her querulousness as fit for a queen.

The Princess and the Pea

RELATIONSHIP RULES,

IN BRIEF

☼ Don't censor your behavior to "land" a man. What if you get him? You're looking at a life of biting your tongue or stifling your laugh—for someone you may not even like.

☼ Know that your inner, important qualities radiate from you, even if a flash flood has flattened your hair and liquefied your mascara, leaving streaks on your cheeks like an extra from *Braveheart*.

☼ Don't take one man's rejection as a reflection of your worth. Different traits attract different people.

☼ Know what you want in a person and wait for someone who has those internal qualities.

Fairy-tale Formula
Rule 2:

Whoever you are,

you are someone's ideal.

Hold out for the person

who sees you as his.

◆ ◆ ◆ ◆ ◆ ◆ ◆ ◆

The supreme happiness of life is the conviction of being loved for yourself, or, more correctly, being loved in spite of yourself.

—VICTOR HUGO, NINETEENTH-CENTURY FRENCH WRITER, AUTHOR OF *LES MISERABLES* AND *THE HUNCHBACK OF NOTRE DAME*

◆ ◆ ◆ ◆ ◆ ◆ ◆ ◆

CHAPTER THREE

The Little Mermaid

(a Tale of Warning)

AQUATIC PRINCESS DROWNS
IN SEA OF UNREQUITED LOVE

he little mermaid—famous for her beauty and mellifluous singing voice—lives with her five sisters and mer-king father in a fabulous palace beneath the sea. But the palace could be a trailer park for all the mermaid cares; she's obsessed with life on land.

One day a terrible storm sinks a royal yacht. The little mermaid sees a beautiful human prince, knocked unconscious, plunging into the roiling ocean. She falls instantly in love with him. She swims through the ship's wreckage, saves his life, and slips back into the sea.

Back home in water world, the little mermaid is despondent, flat on her back in the sand with the force of her love. She knows that humans can't live below water, and that mermaids can't walk on land. Besides, everyone assures her, men don't make passes at scaly-tailed lasses.

Unable to bear her longing for the beautiful prince, she heads to an evil witch for help. The witch offers to slice her tail into legs like a cabaret dancer, if the mermaid will cut out her tongue. Who needs to talk (or sing) when you can walk? So what if each step feels like stepping on glass?

The legs come with another price: If the prince doesn't fall in love with her and marry her, she'll die and turn into sea foam.

When the prince gets a gander at the now-leggy mermaid, he takes her as his constant companion. They go everywhere together—riding, dancing, hiking in the hills. Since she can't talk (or write, or do sign language, apparently), they don't communicate about . . . anything. But she tries to express her thoughts and feelings through her eyes.

For the former mermaid, every day is a combination of joy (she's with the prince!) and pain (each step hurts like hell; she misses her family; is he *ever* going to propose?).

Eventually the prince decides to marry—some human princess who can talk. The little mermaid turns into sea foam.

◆ ◆ ◆ ◆ ◆ ◆ ◆ ◆

"The Little Mermaid," written by Hans Christian Andersen, was first published in 1837. In the Disney version, the little mermaid regains her voice and marries the prince. But Hans Christian Andersen's version has no happy ending. His focuses on the tragedy of unrequited love.

◆ ◆ ◆ ◆ ◆ ◆ ◆ ◆

 The Little Mermaid

THE SAVVY DATER READING

The little mermaid elevated the human world above her own, valuing the foreign more than the known. She took her own assets for granted, unable to appreciate them as much as those beyond her reach.

The little mermaid took unrequited longing to new heights, leaving the depths to do so. Her love for the prince was based on a fantasy of humanity she had cherished her whole life, *not* on real knowledge of him.

The little mermaid didn't give the prince a chance to love her as she was. She could have swum up to the palace and enticed him with her natural charms—her beauty, her expertise in oceanography, her golden hair that flowed like seaweed. But she didn't respect the prince enough to believe he might see past her tail to her true self, and she didn't have enough confidence in her own strengths to try.

And what's with this running to the evil witch the minute things get tough? How many tales end tragically because the heroine acts in a fit of passion, disregarding her family, her friends, and her own belief system?

The little mermaid gave up her singing voice—one of her strongest assets and an essential element of her identity—for a man.

The little mermaid also gave up her speaking voice, believing that hot legs, rather than an emotional and mental connection, are the basis for a strong relationship.

The little mermaid accepted a relationship based on changing herself in an effort to one day "win" a man.

The Little Mermaid

RELATIONSHIP RULES, IN BRIEF

☼ See the beauty and value in your own life. Don't assume it's inferior to your idealized vision of someone else's. The ocean always seems bluer on the other side.

☼ Learn to see someone's interest in you as the supremely attractive trait. How can you really respect someone who doesn't understand how great you are?

☼ If you're lusting after someone who finds one of your essential characteristics, such as your beautiful, iridescent tail, unappealing, he's not the prince for you.

☼ Don't resort to devious tactics in the pursuit of love. If a "strategy" feels wrong to you, it's wrong.

☼ Don't cut off your tongue for anyone! You *cannot* give up your essential strengths for someone else. If a romance would work if you were just a little *less*, swim away.

☼ Attraction is essential, but a lasting relationship also requires real communication and emotional connection.

☼ At least *consider* aiming for someone who comes from a similar enough background that joining together won't force either of you to leave your entire world behind.

Fairy-tale Formula Rule 3:

Don't turn your tail on your

beliefs trying to "win" a man.

It's not a victory if you lose yourself.

The Little Mermaid

ALTERNATIVE READING

Falling in love with a mermaid is like falling in love with a married man, or someone in a committed relationship. Think of yourself as the human princess, and the married man as the mermaid, or merman. The part you love is the human half, what you know and see above the water—that is, when he's with you. But he has an entire life going on under the ocean that you don't see and can't participate in and don't really want to know about. You're looking at his human half and trying to will away everything below the waist.

Your vision of that man does not exist. If he's a merman, he already has a life below the water, and no amount of wishing on your part will change that. He'd have to give up his life, his wife, and his family (if he has kids) to come live with you on land. Even if you present him with a glorious alternative, you're only seeing the human half, the half he shows you. For it to work, there would have to be a way for his fin to become feet without him having to cut out his tongue.

CHAPTER FOUR

The Fairies

POOR GIRL WITH INNER VALUE

SPEAKS AND GROWS RICH IN LOVE

widow has two daughters—an arrogant, lazy older one and a sweet, kind younger one. Mom prefers the bitchy elder; she's a chip off the old block.

One day, when the younger daughter is drawing water at the spring (one of her many chores), an old woman hobbles over, begging for a drink. The girl quickly fills her pitcher from the cleanest part of the spring and holds it up for the thirsty beggar.

. . . who turns out to be a fairy in disguise. The fairy casts a spell on the sweet sister: From now on, whenever she speaks, flowers or jewels will fall from her lips. (This may sound incredibly annoying, but talking in trinkets was considered a remarkable talent at the time.)

Mom is delighted with this new speak-and-grow-rich gift. She sends her favorite daughter off to the spring with explicit instructions to fetch a pail of water for any beggar who appears.

No beggars in sight. Just some socialite-type with perfect hair and plenty of diamonds who claims to be parched. The older daughter refuses to draw water for this lady of leisure. What's in it for her?

A nasty surprise, it turns out. This happens to be the very same fairy in a new disguise, with a new spell: Each time the sour sister speaks, a toad will drop from her lips.

Mom is hopping mad. This is not what she was aiming for. And there are slimy toad-prints on all the furniture! She flies at the younger daughter in a rage, blaming her.

The younger daughter flees to a nearby forest to hide. A local prince, out for a hunt, finds her. He decides that her gift for goody-laden gab is a physical symbol of her giving nature. He brings her home to his castle to be his bride. Happily ever afterness abounds.

Mom and older sister open a snack shack selling French-fried frog legs.

❖ ❖ ❖ ❖ ❖ ❖ ❖ ❖

"The Fairies" is one of the eight tales recorded and published by Charles Perrault. He called the book *Tales of Mother Goose; or Stories from Olden Times,* and included a moral synopsis at the end of each.

❖ ❖ ❖ ❖ ❖ ❖ ❖ ❖

The Fairies

THE SAVVY DATER READING

The younger daughter behaved with dignity in all areas of her life, holding herself to her own personal standard of conduct, even when heading out for another dull day at an obviously dead-end job.

The younger daughter knew she didn't have to be a ball-buster in her personal life to get ahead in her career. She understood that sweetness is the ultimate sign of strength.

She was as kind to the old beggar woman as she would have been to a prince, valuing people over position.

The older daughter shunned the well-dressed woman, viewing kindness only as a means to an end.

Though she came from a poor family, the younger daughter became fabulously rich (and a phenomenon on the talk-show circuit) through her own merit, attracting a prince along the way.

The prince recognized that spewing jewels was not just a bizarre talent but also a physical manifestation of the younger daughter's inner worth—something he valued more than an impressive pedigree.

The Fairies

RELATIONSHIP RULES,
IN BRIEF

☼ Treat everyone with compassion—the unfortunate *and* those who seem to have everything. When it comes to kindness, the means is an end itself.

☼ Never underestimate the power of being sweet.

☼ Don't judge people by appearance alone.

☼ Value yourself for the root of your character, not your family tree. Your prince will do the same.

☼ Hold out for the person who sees your inner beauty so clearly that to him, it's a fact, not his opinion.

◆ ◆ ◆ ◆ ◆ ◆ ◆ ◆

To love someone is to see a miracle invisible to others.

—FRANÇOIS MAURIAC, FRENCH WRITER, 1952 NOBEL PRIZE WINNER FOR LITERATURE

◆ ◆ ◆ ◆ ◆ ◆ ◆ ◆

Fairy-tale Formula
Rule 4:

Hold yourself to your highest

standards no matter how lowly a

particular activity may seem. You

never know how your actions may be

paving the way toward your love.

❖ ❖ ❖ ❖ ❖ ❖ ❖ ❖

The apparently uneventful and stark moment at which our future sets foot in us is so much closer to life than that other noisy and fortuitous point of time at which it happens to us as if from outside . . . and when on some later day it "happens" (that is, steps forth out of us to others), we shall feel in our inmost selves akin and near it . . . that which we call destiny goes forth from within people, not from without into them.

—RAINER MARIA RILKE, FROM *LETTERS TO A YOUNG POET*

❖ ❖ ❖ ❖ ❖ ❖ ❖ ❖

Thumbelina

SINGLE SMALL FEMALE DATES MANY

FROGS, FALLS FOR FLOWER FAIRY

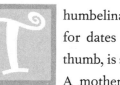humbelina, beautiful though hard-pressed for dates because she's only as big as a thumb, is sleeping in her walnut-shell bed. A mother toad hops into the room and kidnaps her, convinced the tiny girl will make a perfect bride for her son. Thumbelina awakens to find herself trapped on a water lily in the middle of a marsh, face-to-face with a slimy green frog who can't keep his tongue in his mouth and keeps staring at her with bug eyes like he owns her.

Thumbelina escapes the marsh marriage by floating down the river on her lily pad. The current carries her over rapids, around bends, and into another country.

A cockroach swoops down and grabs her, carrying her to cockroach territory in the trees. He's smitten. She's disgusted. There are cockroaches everywhere! The other cockroaches criticize her: "She has only two legs! Such a thin waist!" Passion gives way to peer pressure, and the once-enamored cockroach dumps her.

Thumbelina wanders alone into the forest, convinced she's too ugly even for a cockroach. She strings up a bed, decorates, and learns to live alone in her little hammock in the big woods. Then when winter comes, she nearly dies of frostbite, until she finds refuge with a matronly field mouse in a cozy burrow. Thumbelina tells stories in exchange for room and board.

The field mouse has a rich neighbor, an old mole with a huge subterranean estate connected to the mouse house by an underground passageway. He fixes his tiny eyes on Thumbelina. The field mouse is ecstatic; this is the ideal husband for any girl! He's rich, educated, and get a look at his swanky velvet coat!

Thumbelina doesn't want to marry a mole. But she

puts up with his courting, afraid to insult the mouse. Besides, she can't leave until winter ends.

Meanwhile, she befriends a wounded swallow trapped in the passageway between the two burrows. She spends the winter nursing the swallow back to health. They discover many shared interests—the sunlight, the summer, living *above* the ground.

When summer comes, the swallow invites Thumbelina to fly away with him. She feels too obligated to the field mouse to leave. Instead, she spends the summer sewing her trousseau for her pending marriage.

The day before the big day, Thumbelina heads outside for one last view of the sun (the mole forbids outdoor activity). Just then, the swallow flies overhead, on his way south for the winter. He invites Thumbelina once again. This time she agrees. She climbs on his back and flies away.

. . . to a tropical paradise with a huge sky and brilliant flowers. Here she meets a beautiful prince just her size living in a flower. He has a good job as king of the flower fairies. And he's human (with wings).

Thumbelina and the prince fall instantly in love. The swallow, enamored with Thumbelina all this time, decides that her happiness matters most and settles for remaining good friends.

Thumbelina marries the prince and gets her own set of wings. They live flittingly ever after.

♦ ♦ ♦ ♦ ♦ ♦ ♦ ♦

Written by Hans Christian Andersen, "Thumbelina" is a romantic version of "The Ugly Duckling" (also by Andersen), a story about a superior person (swan) surrounded by people (ducks) who can't appreciate his greatness. Both are stories of journeys toward discovering one's own worth.

♦ ♦ ♦ ♦ ♦ ♦ ♦ ♦

Thumbelina

THE SAVVY DATER READING

The mother toad tried to strand Thumbelina on the water lily to keep her, thinking a good trap was more important than true love.

When her lily pad began careening downstream, Thumbelina didn't cling to the leaf in terror or yearn to be back in the familiarity of the marsh. She was able to enjoy the feeling of free floating and the surprises around each bend. She knew she wouldn't float, untethered, forever.

The cockroach grabbed Thumbelina in a fit of shallow desire. Since he was acting from surface infatuation, not genuine love, he fell out of lust as easily as he fell in it.

The dumped Thumbelina didn't slump miserably among the pine needles, pining away for the right man to rescue her so her "real" life could begin. She knew that if she got in the habit of waiting for someone else to make her happy, misery would become a habit itself, and she'd still be unhappy after her man arrived.

Though the field mouse thought the mole was an ideal husband, Thumbelina had to be true to her own feelings not the mouse's.

Thumbelina's arrangement with the field mouse was mutually beneficial. The mouse saved her life; she made the mouse's life worth living (through her sparkly personality and ability to tell great stories).

Thumbelina fled without saying good-bye. You can bet the mouse was brokenhearted, sure that Thumbelina had been eaten by a cat or squashed by a falling stalk of corn. The mole alternated between grief at her possible death and the sneaking suspicion that maybe she had fled to be free of him. If Thumbelina had been honest with herself—and with them—rather than becoming overwhelmed by misplaced obligation, she could have ended the sham engagement before it started. She would have hurt their feelings briefly, rather than plunging them into years of serious depression and strapping them with huge therapy bills.

Though the swallow wasn't her ultimate love connection, he was an important person (bird) in Thumbelina's life, transporting her out of a bad situation and carrying her to her prince.

When Thumbelina fell for the flower king, she didn't force herself to stay with the swallow. She had learned her lesson back at the mole hole—the reason to be with someone is love, not obligation.

Thumbelina

RELATIONSHIP RULES,
IN BRIEF

☼ You can't force love through limitation.

☼ Ending a relationship, even a bad one, can feel like racing down a rapid river on a lily pad—as if your entire life is careening out of your control. Try to relish the ride. You *will* land on stable ground again.

☼ If a person is enamored of some surface trait (your pretty smile or cool job), he'll lose interest if he doesn't eventually love you for who you are. Don't take it personally. It never was personal. The right man won't leave.

☼ Cultivate the habit of happiness now.

☼ Be honest with yourself about your feelings, even if they seem "wrong" or unkind.

☼ Some men are swallows—catalysts or conduits who fly you to the right man. As long as that relationship is based on genuine concern and care for each other, it is a success—even if it doesn't last forever.

☼ Don't stay in a relationship out of guilt or obligation. If you're unhappy, there's no way your partner is thrilled.

Fairy-tale Formula
Rule 5:

Wait for the person who feels

right to you—not to your friends or

family. Even if it seems like you've

dated every man (and mole) in town,

the right match does exist.

Grace and Derek

BETRAYED PRINCESS LEARNS
TO TRUST AGAIN

 kind and well-educated princess (Grace) learns that her father has just remarried—none other than the Duchess of Grudge, a hideous woman who hates her. Grace has read the fairy tales. She knows the wicked-stepmother routine. Still, she promises her dad she'll be gracious to his wife, then heads to the woods to cry her eyes out alone.

But she's not alone. Who's that handsome man in the stylish slacks? It's Derek, a charming prince with magical powers. Derek declares his undying devotion to Grace and promises to stay near in case of trouble.

Trouble with a capital G. That night, Grudge's soldiers drag Grace deep into a forest full of wild beasts and leave her there to die.

Alone, frightened, swatting endlessly at mosquitoes, Grace calls out to Derek. Suddenly, a lighted pathway appears in the forest. Grace follows it to a glowing palace with crystal walls—Derek's home, magically transported here! Derek invites her in to meet his mom, serves her supper, and gives her a room for the night.

The next morning, Derek asks Grace to marry him. He offers kindness, a Waterford castle, a roomful of clothing just her size and style. But her father is back home, presumably worried sick. Grace, the daughter of duty, heads home.

The king is happy to see her (not that he noticed she was missing). Grace tells her tale of terror in the woods and asks to be sent to a far corner of the kingdom for safety. The king, who has promised Grudge control over Grace, ignores her request and doesn't do a thing.

But Grudge does. That night, after the king is asleep, Grudge locks Grace in a moldy dungeon and demands that she do a series of impossible tasks—or else! First,

Grace must detangle a huge clump of fine fluff and wind it into a ball of thread. Then she must sort a million feathers into tiny packets, according to type of bird.

Ordinarily, Grace is happy to help out around the house. But this is ridiculous. This fluff is so fine, it breaks if you look at it. And not even a bird could tell one feather from another. But Grace doesn't call Derek, too ashamed at having turned down life in a castle for death in the dungeon.

No need. Derek, the prince of perfect timing, suddenly appears. Have wand, will work wonders. Derek transforms the fluff into a ball of strong shipping cable. He sends the feathers flying into separate piles. Then he asks Grace to marry him again.

Now Grace has a new worry. What if Derek doesn't truly love her? How can she trust his love? She thought she could trust her father and look what a mistake that turned out to be.

Disappointed, Derek disappears. Grudge enters, sees Grace's success, and punches her in the face. She didn't want perfect piles. She wanted an excuse to erase Grace!

Now she devises a foolproof plan: Grace must carry a closed box halfway across the kingdom, not opening it, on pain of death. Everyone knows no human can resist the temptation of a closed box. Grace will open it. Voilà! License to kill.

After carrying the box for miles, Grace stops to rest on a rock. What could be in this box, anyway? She decides to peek.

A troupe of tiny dancers and singers leap out. They spin. They waltz. They polka. They're having so much fun, they refuse to go back in the box.

This is it—death for sure. Grace calls Derek, asking him to say good-bye before she dies, if he could still possibly care for someone who would so flagrantly disobey clear instructions.

Derek appears and repacks the little people. Grace once again refuses to marry him, insisting on returning to deliver the box instead.

Grudge is furious when she sees the closed box. She must wipe this pest of perfection off the planet! Having exhausted her well of creative sadism, she decides to push Grace into a huge pit in the ground, cover it with a boulder, and be done with her once and for all.

Buried alive! Grace is about to die from asphyxiation, when a door appears in the side of the pit . . . leading to Derek's crystal castle. Grace finds Derek, apologizes for having been so mistrusting, and says she'll marry him if he still cares for such a silly girl.

Of course he still cares. They get married at once and live chore-free ever after.

◆ ◆ ◆ ◆ ◆ ◆ ◆ ◆

"Grace and Derek," written by the French author Madame d'Aulnoy, was published in *Les Contes des Fées (Tales of Fairies)* in the 1690s. It has many elements found in other tales. The box of tiny people appears in the Russian tale "Baba Yaga."

Both the tiny people and the impossible chores appear in the Italian story "The Girl in the Basket."

Madame d'Aulnoy's own life read like a fairy tale. She was married at age sixteen to a much older man. After having five kids, she plotted to accuse her husband of a crime as a way to free herself from the marriage. When the hoax was discovered, she fled to England and then Spain. King Louis XIV finally pardoned her, allowing her to return to France, where she opened a swanky literary salon and published fairy tales and travel books.

◆ ◆ ◆ ◆ ◆ ◆ ◆

Grace and Derek

THE SAVVY DATER READING

After Grudge abandoned her in a forest full of ferocious beasts, Grace didn't blame her father for his wife's bad behavior, throwing a temper tantrum and demanding that he change his life to suit her needs. Instead, she told him what happened, voiced her concerns about staying around, and offered a solution that would work for both of them—that he send her to a distant domain.

Grace didn't let Grudge's vindictive jealousy drive her to retaliatory revenge plots of her own.

Grace's daughterly devotion was admirable—at first. But when it became obvious that her father wouldn't protect her, her continued loyalty went from righteous to ridiculous. She nearly got herself killed by putting a sense of duty above self-preservation.

Or was it duty? Grace was willing to get punched in the face and return for more, as if she thought she deserved to be punished. But neither Grudge's cruelty nor her father's lack of concern was her fault.

Even though Derek offered a luminous lifestyle and lasting love, Grace didn't trust him. She let her father's betrayal make her suspicious of all men.

Derek not only said he loved Grace, but he also showed her. He introduced her to his family, asked her to marry him, respected her decision not to, rescued her repeatedly (without criticism or condemnation), and knew her taste in clothing and jewels. Grace finally saw that his words and actions matched and she could believe them.

Grace tested Derek's love repeatedly by putting herself in increasingly dangerous situations and waiting for him to save her. She's lucky that Derek was smart enough to realize she was going through a tough time and wouldn't be "testing" him forever.

Grace was sure Derek wouldn't love her anymore after she opened the box. But since Derek's love was genuine, one "mistake" couldn't kill it.

Grace and Derek

RELATIONSHIP RULES,
IN BRIEF

☼ When a problem arises with someone you love, suggest solutions that will work for both of you. Complaints, threats of revenge, and demands of sacrifice rarely solve anything.

☼ Maintain your grace and character, even if those around you seem locked in a competition to see who can make the stupidest choices and commit the meanest acts.

☼ Loyalty must go both ways. Staying with someone at the expense of yourself is staying too long.

☀ Don't blame yourself for someone else's bad behavior. Other people's problems are *never* your fault. Leave the castle before you're buried alive.

☀ Focus your attention on people who value you, not on trying to win the affection of someone who doesn't.

☀ If a person's words and actions match and are consistent over time, it's time to believe him.

☀ You can't test someone's feelings for you forever. Eventually, you'll have to trust him or lose him.

☀ Don't demand proof of "unconditional love" by being your worst possible self. Someone you love deserves you at your best, not your worst.

☀ There is no "one false move" that will drive the right person away.

Fairy-tale Formula
Rule 6:

Don't let a bad experience

with one man make you suspicious

of the next.

All men are *not* alike.

Beauty and the Beast

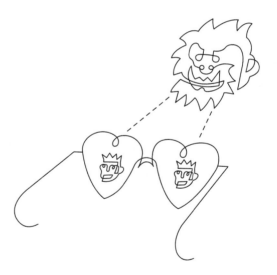

BRAVE-HEARTED BABE SEES PAST

FURRY FACE, FINDS LOVE

 wealthy widower has three daughters. The two oldest spend their days parading around town in head-to-toe Prada, sipping cocktails at the Four Seasons, and shunning all suitors less lofty than a duke. The youngest daughter is not only prettier and nicer, but also deeper, with a sensitivity to fine literature. She is so lovely, everyone calls her "Beauty."

One day, the widower loses all his money. He moves his family to a dilapidated country house upstate. The older sisters are bored out of their minds. There's nothing to do here but look out the windows at the cows and reminisce about their former favorite outfits. Beauty awakens at dawn to help her father, building buff biceps from yard work and developing a beautiful golden tan.

A year later, Dad gets news that his ship has come in (literally). He sets out to the dockyards, amid demands from the greedy sisters for expensive souvenirs—Chanel suits, Gucci bags, Godiva chocolates. Beauty asks for a rose.

The shipload is a bust. (Legal fees eat all his earnings.) Destitute, Dad heads home, but loses his way in a snowstorm. Suddenly, he sees a perfect castle glowing up ahead.

It's like Martha Stewart of the Middle Ages in this castle—rack of mutton served on silver plates, a huge bed hand-stitched by dwarfs, new riding breeches just his size. In the morning, instead of snow, he sees bountiful gardens. That's right! He picks a rose for Beauty.

Suddenly, a terrible beast bolts across the lawn, baring his teeth. The garden is the one thing on earth he loves! Dad pleads for his life, explaining that he's a single parent. The beast lets him live, if one of his daughters will return in his place.

Enter Beauty (after Dad details how her request nearly cost him his life). Instead of eating her, the beast gives her the run of the castle, including her own room with a fully stocked wardrobe and library.

Beauty gets comfortable with castle life. She admits (when pressed) that visually, the beast is pretty revolting. But when she thinks of his kindness, his ugliness seems to fade. If only he wouldn't keep asking her to marry him (an offer she can't help refusing).

Finally, the beast amends his request, asking for lifelong companionship instead. Beauty confesses that as much as she likes living in the castle, she'll never be content away from her father. The beast, wanting her happiness above all else, lets her leave.

Back home at Dad's, Beauty spends her time obsessing about the beast. She can't believe how much she misses him. What's wrong with her? She's not one of those people who only want what they don't have. After dreaming that the beast is dying, she realizes that she does love him after all, even if only as a friend. She rushes back to the castle.

. . . where she finds the beast nearly dead, due to

his efforts to starve himself in her absence. Beauty throws herself on the beast, promising to marry him.

Suddenly, the beast turns into a beautiful prince. And so witty! He was under a spell all this time, condemned to look like a beast until some beautiful girl fell in love with him for his kindness and character alone.

They get married and live happily, and equally attractively, ever after.

◆ ◆ ◆ ◆ ◆ ◆ ◆ ◆

The most popular version of "Beauty and the Beast" was recorded by the French writer Madame Jeanne-Marie de Beaumont and was first published in 1756. Similar tales of a woman condemned to marry a nonhuman suitor are found around the world.

◆ ◆ ◆ ◆ ◆ ◆ ◆ ◆

Beauty and the Beast

THE SAVVY DATER READING

Though Beauty's circumstances kept changing, her unfailing optimism and consistent character helped her thrive wherever she found herself, ultimately leading to her good fortune.

Beauty's father caused all her problems (through his bad business deals, poor sense of direction, and willingness to "guilt" her into going to the beast's castle in his place). But she didn't blame him, claiming that a dysfunctional family excused her from having to be pleasant or happy. She took it upon herself to make her life fulfilling.

Beauty didn't try to change the beast's beastly appearance (pushing him to join a gym, get a makeover, or have his colors done). She acknowledged that his face was a red flag and then dropped it, focusing on his positive traits instead. Fixating on the qualities she admired increased her awareness of these, eventually effacing her sense of his ugly face.

Beauty's main goal at the beast's house was to avoid getting eaten—not to fall in love. But she learned that some people take time to reveal their best selves.

Beauty felt sorry for the beast because of his horrible face. By viewing him with kindness instead of disgust or anger, she began paving the way for falling in love.

The beast didn't hold his claws close to his chest, waiting to confess his love until she confessed hers. He knew that hiding his feelings would not protect him from getting hurt.

Though Beauty and the beast seemed opposite externally, they had an essential inner compatibility (as evidenced by their mutual love of roses).

Beauty is damn lucky that the beast was really a handsome, smart prince in disguise. It's one thing to admire a man's inner qualities; it's another to marry someone who doesn't excite you, who doesn't make you want to wake up in the morning just so you can touch him.

The beast is lucky Beauty returned when she did. In another few days, he would have been dead, and she would have been devastated.

Beauty and the Beast

RELATIONSHIP RULES,
IN BRIEF

☀ Never underestimate the power of a positive outlook.

☀ A strong moral center is your best protection against bad fortune and is the source of your good luck.

☀ Take responsibility for your own happiness, wherever you find yourself.

☼ Not everyone makes a dazzling first impression. Give people a chance to reveal their most beautiful sides.

◆ ◆ ◆ ◆ ◆ ◆ ◆ ◆

We attract hearts by the qualities we display; we retain them by the qualities we possess.

—JEAN SUARD, FRENCH WRITER

◆ ◆ ◆ ◆ ◆ ◆ ◆ ◆

☼ Don't obsess about your lover's "flaws." Fixating on problems intensifies them and gives them more strength, the way watering a plant helps it grow. Mention your concerns, then drop them. Pay attention to the traits you *do* admire instead. Either the "flaws" will fade out of sight or they will be the reasons you'll break up.

☀ View your lover's "faults" with compassion, not condemnation.

☀ Express your affection. Saving face is not the same as saving your feelings.

☀ A good relationship requires genuine compatibility.

☀ Don't agree to marry someone, secretly hoping that your commitment will change him. This only happens in fairy tales.

☀ Do *not* starve yourself to death because you're craving a particular person's love. Never give up on your life because someone else can't see its value.

Fairy-tale Formula
Rule 7:

Focus on seeing the best in people,

not the worst.

You never know how a relationship

will evolve.

Bluebeard

(a Tale of Warning)

GOLD DIGGER MARRIES FOR MONEY,

NEARLY DIGS OWN GRAVE

wealthy bachelor wants to marry one of his neighbor's pretty daughters—he doesn't care which one. Both girls refuse, repulsed by his ratty-looking blue beard and the fact that he's already had three wives, and no one knows what happened to them.

Still, the girls accept an invitation to a weeklong party at one of his ranches. Eight days of drinking, horseback riding, and off-road racing later, the youngest daughter decides that his beard isn't so blue after all. True, she's too hungover to see straight, but who cares that he has a stringy goatee like a roadie for ZZ Top when you're having this much fun? She agrees to marry Bluebeard the next week.

Married life is golden—so many cars, so much furniture. A month later, Bluebeard has to leave on business. He gives his new wife the keys to all his possessions, telling her she can do whatever she wants, except enter the little room in the basement. She promises to follow his wishes.

But her curiosity is stronger than her commitment. Bluebeard barely leaves the building before she's down the stairs, jiggling the key in the lock. She flings open the door, revealing a dark room with sticky stuff all over the floor. Is that blood? Yes! And those things swaying on the walls? Corpses! They're the bodies of Bluebeard's previous wives, hanging, throats cut.

Horrified, the still-living (though barely breathing) wife drops the key in a pool of clotted blood. She grabs it, slams the door, and runs upstairs. Back in her room, sitting on her three-hundred-count Egyptian cotton sheets, she notices some blood on the key. She tries to wipe it off, but it's stuck like red paint.

Bluebeard returns that night, sees the bloody key, and guesses what happened. Purple with fury, he climbs the stairs to her room. She has betrayed him! He knew he couldn't trust her! He grabs her by the hair, raising his cutlass to her throat.

Suddenly, her two brothers race up to the mansion. They see what's about to happen and kill Bluebeard instead.

The new bride–turned–new widow inherits Bluebeard's money. And a horror of locked rooms.

* * * * * * * *

Bluebeard was one of the stories recorded by Charles Perrault. No one knows who the tale is based on exactly. It may be modeled after a French nobleman, Gilles de Rais, who murdered more than a hundred people, or Britain's King Henry VIII, known for killing two of his six wives.

* * * * * * * *

Bluebeard

THE SAVVY DATER READING

The youngest daughter fell in love with Bluebeard's belongings, not with him. She learned, nearly too late, that she had married the man, not merely his mansions.

The youngest daughter entrusted her life to a stranger without bothering to get to know him well enough to make sure this was a good idea. She put her life in the hands of a murderer, nearly losing it in the process.

Yes, it's horrifying to find your husband's previous wives murdered and strung up to die, but the new wife promised not to enter the room. She knew she lacked the self-restraint to resist such a temptation; she should have turned to him for assistance—asking him to take the key with him, for example. They were supposed to be partners in this marriage. If she felt comfortable enough to marry him, she should have felt comfortable enough to ask him for help meeting his needs.

Not that Bluebeard was the ideal husband. He had already murdered three relationships through his obsessive need to make his wives prove their love. No wonder he had doubts. He wooed his wives with property and parties, wedding women attracted to his purchasing power, not his personality.

Of course his new wife looked in the locked room. Three out of three of his previous wives had done the exact same thing. What did he *think* was going to happen this time? Rather than learning from his mistakes, he tried the same test-and-murder approach to marriage once again.

Bluebeard accuses his wife of being disloyal, but how devoted was he, far more interested in tricking her into betraying him than in protecting her from the horrifying sight of three dead women strung up on the wall?

◆ ◆ ◆ ◆ ◆ ◆ ◆ ◆

If you would be loved, love and be lovable.

—BENJAMIN FRANKLIN

◆ ◆ ◆ ◆ ◆ ◆ ◆ ◆

Bluebeard

RELATIONSHIP RULES,
IN BRIEF

☼ Don't confuse a fondness for home furnishings with feelings of genuine affection. You marry a person, not his possessions.

☼ Just because a man wants you and matches your checklist of desires does *not* mean he's right for you. Assess his character, not his qualifications.

☼ Assume the best of everyone, but don't rely on that assumption until you've had time to ensure it's true. Get to know a person *before* entrusting him with anything you can't afford to lose— such as your happiness.

☼ A relationship is a team effort. Turn to your partner first for help solving problems between the two of you.

☼ Don't do a Bluebeard when looking for love. Attracting someone by flashing your credentials or cash leaves you doubting his affection. Is it you or your Mercedes? The right person will fall for you, not for your car or career or country club.

☼ If one approach to creating closeness continues to fail, try a new tack.

☼ Loyalty and trust develop over time, by being loyal and trustworthy yourself.

Fairy-tale Formula
Rule 8:

Don't make people prove
their love. Commitment tests
and truth traps create suspicion,
never devotion.

CHAPTER NINE

The Fisherman and His Wife

(a Tale of Warning)

MATERIAL GIRL SEEKS CONSUMER

SOLUTION TO MISERABLE MARRIAGE

 fisherman and his wife live in a ditch by the sea. He spends his days casting for cod; she, hanging around the hut, wishing she'd hooked a better husband.

One day, he reels in a talking fish. The chatty catch explains that he's actually an enchanted prince and begs to be released. The fisherman, loath to eat a prince-turned-pickerel anyway, agrees.

But his wife doesn't. Everyone knows that magic fishes grant wishes. She sends her husband back to the sea to ask the fish for a cottage.

Holy mackerel! The fisherman returns to find his shack transformed into a Cape Cod–style cabin with gray shingles, white shutters, and a courtyard full of ducks and chickens. Finally, something to eat besides fish! The fisherman is very happy. His wife is moderately happy. Everything goes swimmingly.

. . . for about a week. But then the fisherman's wife decides that a cottage is too confining. They need a castle to be comfortable. She sends her husband to ask for one.

Great tuna! The fisherman returns to a huge stone castle with dozens of rooms and towering turrets. Outside there are even more things to eat—goats, cows, deer, a garden full of heirloom vegetables and shiitake mushrooms. There's enough here to be happy for life.

His wife isn't so sure. What good is a castle if you're not king? The next morning, she tells her husband to ask the fish to make her king.

The fisherman hems and haws. He hangs around the castle, making up excuses. What if the fish gets angry? His wife insists the fish will submit and sends him out the door.

Sure enough, the fisherman returns to find his wife seated on a diamond throne, sporting a golden crown.

But the thrill is already gone. Now she wants to be emperor. The fisherman refuses. Enough is enough. The tide of their luck is bound to turn. His wife points to her crown, reminds him that he is her subject, and sends him out the door.

Back to the sea. Then back to the castle—where the fisherman finds his wife high atop an emperor's throne, surrounded by dozens of manservants and a fleet of snappy soldiers. She has a huge crown two yards high (and a horrible headache from all that weight).

But something else is bothering her. That night, she lies awake, tossing and turning. When the sun rises, she realizes the problem. She must be lord of the sun and the moon! Of course. Go ask the fish!

There's a huge storm raging at sea. The fisherman trembles so much, the fish can barely hear what he's saying. But when he does understand, he finally flips.

. . . and grants his own wish. The fisherman returns home to find his wife back in the original ditch. They live muddily ever after.

◆ ◆ ◆ ◆ ◆ ◆ ◆ ◆

"The Fisherman and His Wife" was recorded by the Grimm brothers. Actual brothers, Jacob Ludwig Carl Grimm and Wilhelm Carl Grimm were librarians in Germany who decided to collect and record the traditional oral folk tales of Germany before they were forgotten. They published two hundred of these tales in two volumes in 1812 and 1814. There are many parallels between the Grimms' "German" fairy tales and those found in France and other parts of the world.

◆ ◆ ◆ ◆ ◆ ◆ ◆ ◆

The Fisherman and His Wife

THE SAVVY DATER READING

The fisherman and his wife were caught in a miserable marriage. He ignored his unhappiness by staying away from home, she by attempting to fill the void with manic materialism and crazed ambition.

The new digs delighted the fisherman and his wife only briefly, and for a shorter amount of time with each move.

The fisherman didn't want to keep pestering the prince for a better address. But rather than telling his wife his opinion and backing it up with solid, thoughtful reasons, he created flimsy excuses—weak objections she easily overrode.

The fisherman's wife not only wore the pants in that marriage (as well as the shoes and shirt), but she also held the purse strings and controlled the car keys.

The fisherman's wife may have been a greedy, ambition-crazed shark, but at least she had creativity and drive—characteristics the fisherman sorely lacked. If they had combined their strengths, they could have improved their situation (as she envisioned) and quit while they were ahead (as he advised).

There was a sea of difference between the fisherman and his wife in terms of ambition, drive, values, lifestyle choices, personality, and style. Had they been more equally paired, they would have had a better chance at happiness.

The Fisherman and His Wife

RELATIONSHIP RULES,
IN BRIEF

☀ Don't think that ignoring problems will make them disappear.

☀ A physical change, such as moving to a different house, may temporarily improve a troubled relationship—but not for long. Distractions cannot strengthen a weak foundation.

☀ State your opinions and support them with logical points, not watery excuses.

☼ Make your relationship a partnership, not a dictatorship. If one person calls all the shots, you're both going to miss the target.

☼ Differing strengths can lead to a stronger union. Make room for both people's skills.

☼ Your perfect catch is someone who shares your values and general lifestyle desires.

❖ ❖ ❖ ❖ ❖ ❖ ❖ ❖

Give me a cave up in the mountains,
Or a shack down by the sea.
And I will be in heaven, honey,
If you are there with me.

—ELVIS PRESLEY, SINGING "ANYPLACE IS PARADISE,"
WRITTEN BY JOE THOMAS

❖ ❖ ❖ ❖ ❖ ❖ ❖ ❖

Fairy-tale Formula Rule 9:

Don't fish for material solutions

to relationship problems.

No amount of money makes up

for a mediocre match.

CHAPTER TEN

Sleeping Beauty

ONE-HUNDRED-SIXTEEN-YEAR-OLD
WOMAN FINDS LOVE AT LAST

 childless royal couple finally has a baby. They throw a huge party, inviting everyone they know, including seven fairies reported to give good gifts. They completely forget about an eighth, older, irritable fairy everyone assumes is dead since she's been incommunicado for the past fifty years.

The old fairy, alive and kicking with spite, crashes the party. She rants and raves about not having her own golden dinner plate like all the other fairies. In a fit of horrendous manners and hurt feelings, she casts a spell on the baby, condemning her to prick her hand on a spindle and die.

The youngest fairy commutes the curse, saying the pricked princess will fall asleep for a hundred years instead. The king instantly orders removal of all spindles from the kingdom. Still, no one feels much like dancing, and the party breaks up early.

Life spins along normally for the next sixteen or so years. One day, the princess discovers an old woman working on a spinning wheel in a garret right in the castle. The princess asks to try.

Of course she pricks her hand. Instant slumber. The youngest fairy puts the rest of the court to sleep as well. A huge forest instantly springs up around the castle to protect them.

Flash forward a hundred years. A young prince sees castle spires peeking up above the forest. He cuts through the underbrush, discovering the sleeping princess inside the castle. She awakens, gets one look at the prince, and declares that he's the man she's been dreaming about for the past hundred years. He can't help noticing that she's decked out in some kind of Total Vintage Collection and that her court musicians seem perpetually stuck on golden oldies hour. Still, they talk for hours, fall in love, and get married on the spot.

But the prince doesn't bring Sleeping Beauty back home to meet the folks. He hides his marriage from his parents, spending the next two years running back and forth between the two castles, lying about his activities like some high school sophomore who just discovered alcohol.

When his dad dies, the prince finally brings Sleeping Beauty—and the two children they've now had—home to meet his mother. Then he heads off to war, leaving mom in charge.

Mom, who happens to be half ogre, decides to eat Sleeping Beauty and the kids. The cook hides the family, serving Mom delicious woodland creatures instead. When Mom discovers the switch, she decides to throw everyone into a huge pot of famished vipers and sauté them all for supper.

Just then, the prince returns. Caught in the act of trying to fry his family (and the best cook they've had in years), Mom flings herself into the pot instead. Sleeping Beauty and the prince live happily, though psychologically scarred, ever after.

❖ ❖ ❖ ❖ ❖ ❖ ❖ ❖

The version of "Sleeping Beauty" complete with the ogre mother was recorded by Charles Perrault. The Sleeping Beauty story is believed to date back at least to the fourteenth century.

❖ ❖ ❖ ❖ ❖ ❖ ❖ ❖

Sleeping Beauty

THE SAVVY DATER READING

The king and queen say they thought the evil fairy was dead because they hadn't heard from her in fifty years. But the phone (or carrier pigeon or fleet-footed messenger boy) works both ways. They knew she lacked social savvy; they could have called her. By only including the hipper, more pleasant fairies in their lives, they let a difficult relationship devolve into disaster.

Though the king spared no expense trying to save Sleeping Beauty—issuing a recall on wooden spindles, putting hundreds of wood carvers out of work and devastating the local textile trade—he learned that no parent can keep his child cloistered forever.

Though Sleeping Beauty had been out of circulation for a hundred years, she wasn't afraid to pursue a relationship once she woke up. True, her clothes were outdated, she knew none of the latest recording artists, and she was completely oblivious to the political issues facing the kingdom. But she and the prince still found plenty to talk about and enough common ground for falling in love.

Even though he was a husband and father, the prince acted like a child, hiding his wife from his parents and giving his mother, instead of his spouse, authority over his kingdom. His immaturity and misplaced priorities made him nearly lose his wife and children—and did, ultimately, cause him to lose his mother.

Sleeping Beauty

RELATIONSHIP RULES,
IN BRIEF

☀ Reach out to family members—even the annoying ones. Cutting communication not only alienates those who should be your closest allies, but also distances you from important parts of yourself.

☀ Your parents or friends can't protect you from your own life experiences, even though they'll try. Don't criticize yourself for not learning from others' mistakes.

☀ It may seem like you've been single for one hundred years, but that doesn't mean you'll be single forever.

☼ Have the courage to reenter the dating world, no matter how long you've been away. Essential ways of connecting with others don't change.

☼ Take responsibility for including your parents in your new relationship by finding new roles for them. Make your spouse your priority, but don't pit him against your relatives.

Fairy-tale Formula
Rule 10:

Don't give up on love,

even if it seems like you've been single

for one hundred years. The length of

time it takes is no reflection

on your worth or appeal.

❖ ❖ ❖ ❖ ❖ ❖ ❖ ❖

He does not wait too long who waits for something good.

—Queen Christina of Sweden to Prince Karl Gustav, in the seventeenth century

❖ ❖ ❖ ❖ ❖ ❖ ❖ ❖

The Fairy-tale Formula Top Ten Rules Recap

☼ Don't let past bad luck cloud your vision of a brighter future. Have the courage to believe in a better life. ("Cinderella")

☼ Whoever you are, you are someone's ideal. Hold out for the person who sees you as his. ("The Princess and the Pea")

☼ Don't turn your tail on your beliefs trying to "win" a man. It's not a victory if you lose yourself. ("The Little Mermaid")

☼ Hold yourself to your highest standards no matter how lowly a particular activity may seem. You never know how your actions may be paving the way toward your love. ("The Fairies")

☀ Wait for the person who feels right to you—not to your friends or family. Even if it seems like you've dated every man (and mole) in town, the right match does exist. ("Thumbelina")

☀ Don't let a bad experience with one man make you suspicious of the next. All men are not alike. ("Grace and Derek")

☀ Focus on finding the best in people, not the worst. You never know how a relationship will evolve. ("Beauty and the Beast")

☀ Don't make people prove their love. Commitment tests and truth traps create suspicion, never devotion. ("Bluebeard")

☀ Don't fish for material solutions to relationship problems. No amount of money makes up for a mediocre match. ("The Fisherman and His Wife")

☼ Don't give up on love, even if it seems like you've been single for one hundred years. The length of time it takes is no reflection on your worth or appeal. ("Sleeping Beauty")

epilogue

his book is not just a formula for *finding* love, but also for making love last. Even Cinderella, the original lucky-in-love woman, couldn't abandon her character once she slid into that glass slipper. Yes, she landed the prince, but she also landed herself smack in the center of a court full of ladies who had their own hearts set on her new husband. Who knows what kind of social isolation she had to endure? The gossip. The back-stabbing. The slights at her poor education and career history. And talk about differences! Cinderella had more in common with her handmaid than with her husband. Speaking of her

Prince Charming, how self-absorbed do you suppose he was, having grown up in a castle full of sycophantic subjects catering to his every whim? Another woman (one of her stepsisters, for example) would have destroyed that relationship with unrelenting complaints.

The fact is, there is no *one* suitor or situation guaranteed to lead to eternal bliss; it's up to you to create your own happy ending. Fortunately, you know how to do it. The characteristics that make you the belle of the dating ball are many of the same ones that lead to a lasting love: Allowing your relationship to evolve according to its unique characteristics rather than comparing it to some idealized external image. Seeing the best in your partner and your situation. Making the most of what may come your way. Holding fast to your own ideals. Being kind first and asking questions later.

Every time I reread these tales, I notice new "rules," ones that apply to issues I'm thinking about at the moment. I hope you'll use this book in the same way. Don't abandon these tales like some ragged-eared Cliffs

Notes from freshman lit once you're done dating. You may marry a perfect prince from some idyllic island nation, but your happiness is still in your hands. Continue to look to these optimistic women for inspiration and to follow their lead by letting your most noble side shine.